Ben Passman's

Job Interview Guide

Crossing the Threshold

to your Dream Job

This book is for bold trailblazers who dare to dream. It's for the wide-eyed children still full of wonder, may you stay curious enough to reach for the stars. It's for those feeling stuck on autopilot, rekindle your inner fire and take the wheel towards new horizons. It's for the restless souls yearning for more, your purpose is ready to be uncovered. Your inner compass knows the way. Chart your course by the stars that spark your spirit. Let your childhood dreams and unrestrained imagination guide you once more. Blaze your own trail. Walk the untrodden path with your heart as your light. Success will meet you there, for it lives in the space where your gifts and joy ignite.

This book opens the door to your dream job.

CONTENTS

INTRODUCTION

Landing a new job is exciting but also nerve-wracking. Interviews can feel intimidating, but proper preparation is key. In Ben Passman's Job Interview Guide, you'll learn strategies and best practices to help you ace any job interview with confidence.

This comprehensive guide covers everything from research to follow-up. You'll learn how to thoroughly research the company and role so you can tailor your responses. You will learn the secret to taking control of the interview and uncovering the topics most important to the organization. We discuss how to anticipate common interview questions and practice articulating compelling, thoughtful answers. Additionally, you'll get tips on presenting yourself professionally—from dress code to handshake etiquette.

This guide also provides advice to help you stand out, like asking smart questions and sending prompt thank you notes. You'll get an insider perspective on what impresses interviewers and makes candidates shine. With these tips, you can walk into any interview feeling self-assured and ready to make a great impression.

Whether you're fresh out of college or a seasoned professional, Ben Passman's Job Interview Guide will give you the tools to successfully navigate any job interview. By the end, you'll have the knowledge and confidence to impress any interviewer and land your dream job. So read on to learn the strategies that will get you hired!

Chapter 1 – So, You Landed an Interview?

Congratulations, you got the call to schedule an interview! This exciting milestone means your resume stood out and the hiring manager sees potential in your candidacy. Now it's time to take the next steps and continue making a fantastic impression.

When the company reaches out to schedule the interview, respond promptly to confirm your availability. Provide a few options for days and times that work well for you. However, avoid saying "I'm totally open" or "Anytime is fine" - this sounds potentially desperate rather than accommodating.

If the proposed date/time doesn't work, politely propose an alternate such as "Tuesday morning would be perfect, but unfortunately I have a conflict that Wednesday. Would Thursday at 10am be a possibility instead?" Offering a specific alternative shows flexibility.

In your reply, express enthusiasm about the opportunity to meet and share more about your experience. For example, "Thank you for extending an invitation to learn more about this promising role."

When confirming logistics, don't assume any details like the interviewer's name, location, or video call links. Politely ask the scheduler to provide full specifics so you have the right information.

Following up with a thank you email to the scheduler reiterates your appreciation and professionalism. This sets a positive tone leading into the interview experience.

With prompt, thoughtful replies and polite inquiries about scheduling particulars, you'll confirm your spot while making a great impression. The interview is your time to shine - seize the opportunity!

When her phone lit up with an email from one of her target dream jobs, Jen could barely contain her excitement. They wanted to schedule an interview for the project manager role she had applied for! Jen knew she needed to respond thoughtfully and promptly.

Jen politely replied the same day thanking them for the opportunity. She suggested Tuesday or Friday morning for the interview since her schedule was flexible those days. She also offered times the following week to make it easier for the recruiter if necessary.

The recruiter replied proposing Tuesday at 10am. Jen responded confirming her availability at that exact time. Since the email didn't specify further details, Jen asked to kindly provide the interviewer's name, office location or Zoom link, and any other instructions ahead of time.

The recruiter thanked Jen for the quick response and provided the missing details, including a calendar invitation. To reaffirm her enthusiasm, Jen replied, "Can't wait to meet with Julie next Tuesday to discuss the team dynamics and the responsibilities of the role in more detail."

The day before the interview, Jen sent the recruiter a brief email expressing her appreciation again for scheduling and her excitement for the meeting.

When Tuesday arrived, Jen felt completely prepared and ready to interview successfully. Her prompt, thoughtful replies and polite requests for details had kicked off the process positively. She had followed each step of the "interview scheduling chess match" flawlessly so far.

<u>Here are some ideas to help you get started:</u>

- Respond to the interview invitation promptly - within 24 hours ideally.
- Provide 2-3 options of days/times you are available. Avoid saying "anytime works."
- If the proposed time doesn't work, politely suggest a specific alternative day/time.
- Express enthusiasm and appreciation for the opportunity in your response.
- Request the interviewer's name, location, and any other logistics you need.
- Add the interview to your calendar once details are confirmed.
- Follow up with the scheduler by email to reaffirm your appreciation.
- Research the interviewer and role again as the date approaches.
- Plan your interview attire.
- Send a brief email the day before to express your continued excitement.
- Show up! Completely. Don't hot dog the interview.

Chapter 2 - No one likes homework...

One of the most important things you can do to prepare for a job interview is conduct thorough research on the company and specific role. This demonstrates your genuine interest and helps you craft tailored responses that impress hiring managers.

Start by visiting the company's website and reading all about their history, mission, values, leadership team, products/services, culture, and current challenges. Look for any press releases or news articles about the company as well. Get a sense of the company's brand and what makes them unique.

Next, dig into the specific job description. Make sure you understand the day-to-day responsibilities and qualifications. Look up any terms or software programs you don't recognize. Being familiar with the role shows you did your homework.

It can also be insightful to browse the LinkedIn profiles of people who currently have the role you're applying for. This gives you a sense of the typical background and career path. Reach out to any connections who work for the company to gain an insider perspective.

Research will reveal key facts, statistics, and anecdotes about the company that you can reference to demonstrate your knowledge. For example, maybe the company recently expanded to 10 new locations - you could ask how the interviewer has managed that growth. This illustrates that you know what's going on and are interested in the company's challenges and successes.

Come prepared with thoughtful questions that show you understand the company's goals and priorities. Ask the interviewer for more details on something you researched that intrigued you. Questions should demonstrate curiosity, not ignorance.

With diligent research, you can craft compelling stories and responses tailored specifically for this role and company. This effort will distinguish you from other candidates and convey sincere passion.

My friend Jeremy was thrilled when he received an invitation to interview for his dream job as a product manager at Microsoft. This was a huge opportunity, but Jeremy knew he would be competing with many qualified candidates.

Determined to stand out, Jeremy spent hours thoroughly researching Microsoft and the product manager role. He poured through their website to understand Microsoft's company history, vision, products, culture, and executive bios. He read recent news articles profiling Microsoft's rapid growth and sustained place in the technology sector. Jeremy even looked up Microsoft employees on LinkedIn to review their backgrounds.

One VP who would be interviewing Jeremy had a similar career path, starting in engineering roles before transitioning to leadership. Jeremy took note of this.

Jeremy also analyzed the job description carefully. He researched unfamiliar software programs listed in the requirements so he could speak intelligently about them.

When interview day arrived, Jeremy's preparation paid off. He wove in an anecdote about Microsoft's origins that he had read about. The interviewers were impressed.

When asked about his technical experience, Jeremy highlighted a past project using one of the same programs Microsoft relied on. The VP remarked "Perfect, you already know our solutions - that will help you hit the ground running here."

By doing his homework, Jeremy could speak Microsoft's language and make connections. His research helped him craft tailored responses that conveyed his passion. Two weeks later, Jeremy received the call offering him the job. His diligent preparation had made all the difference in standing out from the pack.

<u>Here are some activities to help you get started:</u>

- Visit the company website and read up on their history, mission, leadership, products, culture, recent news. Get a feel for their brand.
- Google the company and look for recent news articles profiling developments, growth, challenges.
- Search for employees on LinkedIn to understand typical backgrounds and qualifications for the role.
- Analyze the job description in detail - research any unfamiliar requirements.
- Make a list of key facts, stats, anecdotes from your research to reference.

Chapter 3 - Practice Makes Perfect.

While you can't predict every question you'll be asked in an interview, there are many common and expected questions that you can prepare for ahead of time.

Start by brainstorming likely questions about your specific background, experience, skills, and interests. Expect interviewers to ask, "tell me about yourself" or "walk me through your resume." Be ready to concisely walk through your background and career highlights. Focus on experiences and accomplishments that are most relevant to the role.

Also prepare to answer, "why are you interested in this position?" Share your research and your genuine enthusiasm for the company's mission and products or services. Make specific connections between your skills and interests and the role's responsibilities.

To demonstrate self-awareness, prepare to answer questions about your strengths and weaknesses. Pick strengths directly related to the role and pick weaknesses that are not central to the job. Then, share how you're working to improve in areas of weakness.

Other common questions include:

- Why did you leave your last job? Focus on positive reasons like seeking new growth opportunities.
- Where do you see yourself in 5 years? Align your goals with the company's objectives.
- Why should we hire you? Summarize your most relevant qualifications and skills.

Practice answering questions out loud until your delivery sounds natural, not rehearsed. Ask a friend to conduct a mock interview with you to practice in a realistic setting. Preparing thorough answers to expected questions will prevent you from being caught off guard.

During the interview, listen closely to each question asked, and pause briefly to collect your thoughts if needed. You've got this!

Natalie was eager for her upcoming final interview for a social media manager role at an advertising agency. She knew nailing the interview questions would be key to getting hired.

The night before, Natalie wrote down likely questions based on her research of the company and role. She brainstormed how she would concisely walk through her social media experience. Natalie prepared an explanation for why she left her previous agency. She came up with a list of her strongest skills that matched the position's needs.

Natalie practiced out loud with her roommate to polish her delivery. Her roommate also asked unexpected questions to keep Natalie on her toes.

The next day, Natalie felt confident and ready. The interviewer asked "tell me about yourself" right away. Natalie smoothly summarized her background and qualifications.

When asked "why are you interested in this role?" Natalie emphasized her passion for the agency's mission and client brands. She highlighted several innovative social campaigns they had done that inspired her.

The interviewer smiled and said, "It's great to hear you know our work so well." At the end, when asked, "Why should we hire you?" Natalie summarized her impressive social media results. Two days later she received the call with the job offer. Her preparation had clearly paid off.

<u>Here are some activities to help you get started:</u>

- Make a list of likely interview questions based on the job description.
- Practice answering "tell me about yourself" succinctly, focusing on relevant experiences.
- Prepare a response explaining why you're interested in the company and role specifically.
- Identify 2-3 strengths aligned with the role; pick 1 weakness unrelated to core duties.
- Rehearse explaining why you left a previous job positively.
- Craft an answer to, "why should we hire you?" summarizing key qualifications.
- Practice answering questions aloud until responses sound natural.
- Enlist a friend to conduct a mock interview with potential curveball questions.

Chapter 4 – Gameplan.

The interview is a two-way conversation, so you should prepare in advance some thoughtful questions to ask the hiring manager. Asking smart questions demonstrates your engagement and interest in the role and company.

Some examples of good questions to ask include:

- What are the most immediate challenges someone in this role would need to address? Shows you are thinking about how to have an impact.
- How would you describe the culture here? Get insight into values, communication styles, and collaboration.
- What performance goals would you have for someone in this role in the first 3 months? Reveals what they prioritize for success.
- What training, mentorship, or development opportunities are available? Demonstrates your interest in continuously improving.
- What do you enjoy most about working here? Provides perspective on work/life balance.

Avoid questions that could easily be researched or seem too obvious. Also refrain from asking about salary, benefits, or vacation time too early.

Questions should demonstrate your understanding of the company and role while seeking deeper insight from the interviewer's perspective. Smart questions require thoughtful preparation just like your answers. With good questions, you can engage in an insightful discussion that leaves a memorable impression.

Tyler had his final interview for a project manager role at a construction company. He knew that asking intelligent questions was key to standing out.

The night before, Tyler prepared open-ended questions based on his research. He wanted to gain deeper insights from the hiring manager's perspective.

When asked, "Do you have any questions for me?" towards the end of the interview, Tyler pulled out his notebook.

He asked about priorities and challenges for someone new to this role. The manager appreciated Tyler's interest in making an immediate impact. She described upcoming projects that would require sharp focus starting day one.

Tyler also asked thoughtful questions about company culture, training programs, and her own career path. The interviewer remarked that Tyler asked excellent questions that showed his engagement.

After the interview, the manager told the CEO, "I was impressed by the way Tyler took the time to prepare thoughtful questions. He will come in ready to dive right into the most pressing projects."

Within a few days, Tyler received the call with the job offer. Asking intelligent, researched questions had demonstrated Tyler's passion and critical thinking skills. His preparation had paid off once again.

Here are some activities to help you get started:

- Research the company's current goals, challenges, and priorities.
- Prepare a list of 5-6 open-ended questions that demonstrate interest.
- Inquire about immediate challenges someone new would need to tackle.
- Ask for details about company culture and values.
- Find out specific performance goals expected for the role.
- Ask about training, mentoring and professional development opportunities.
- Get the interviewer's perspective - what do they enjoy most about working there.
- Practice asking questions aloud to polish delivery.
- Bring your list of questions in a padfolio or notebook.
- Actively listen and ask thoughtful follow-up questions.
- Share your own experiences or perspectives when relevant.
- Take notes if helpful - jot down key points.

Chapter 5 - Suit Up!

The way you present yourself physically is an important aspect of any job interview. Dressing professionally makes a strong first impression and conveys you are taking the interview seriously.

The standard guideline for an interview is business attire. That means, use your best judgement. Know your industry standard. As they say, when in Rome...

Avoid bold patterns or distracting accessories. Simple jewelry like a watch or plain earrings is fine. Make sure clothes are neatly pressed - wrinkles look sloppy.

Shoes should be polished dress shoes that complement your outfit. Avoid anything too casual like sneakers or open-toed shoes. Even for video interviews, wear a complete outfit.

Pay close attention to personal grooming as well. Hair should be clean and neatly styled. Shave or neatly trim any facial hair. Keep makeup simple and natural looking. Brush teeth and use mouthwash before the interview.

In general, err on the side of being a little overdressed rather than underdressed. It's better to be more formal than not formal enough. If you're unsure, call and ask about the office dress code ahead of time.

Looking polished and professional for the interview sends the message that you take this opportunity seriously. Proper attire paired with confident body language will help you make a great first impression.

Jasmine had a final stage interview for a corporate analyst role at a respected finance firm. She knew the company had a formal work environment.

The night before, Jasmine selected a tailored navy suit with a crisp white button-down shirt. She made sure it was neatly pressed with no wrinkles. Jasmine chose simple pearl earrings and classic pumps to complete the look.

On interview day, Jasmine arrived focused and professionally polished. The hiring manager greeted her warmly and complimented her style.

During the interview, Jasmine's well-groomed hairstyle and neat attire allowed her to focus completely on the conversation. She spoke confidently with engaging body language.

One week later, Jasmine received the official job offer. During the conversation, the manager remarked "Your qualifications are outstanding, and your professional polish left a fantastic impression." Her diligent preparation on attire and grooming had complemented her smooth interview performance perfectly. Jasmine was glad she took the time to learn the company culture and dress appropriately, it was key for landing her dream finance role.

<u>Here are some activities to help you get started:</u>

- Research the company dress code and work environment ahead of time.
- Select professional, polished interview attire that aligns with the company culture.
- Iron or steam clothes to avoid wrinkles.
- Shine dress shoes and keep accessories simple.
- Neatly style your hair and groom any facial hair.
- Apply natural-looking professional makeup.
- Make sure your suit is well-fitted and ties coordinate.
- Inspect your outfit in a mirror before the interview.
- Bring a breath mint and lip gloss to refresh yourself.
- Arrive early to use the restroom to check your appearance.
- During the interview, sit tall with confident body language.

Chapter 6 – Make Friends with the Cooks.

Being punctual and arriving early to a job interview is essential to making a great first impression.

For in-person interviews, plan to arrive 10-15 minutes early. Account for factors like travel time, parking, stopping at the restroom to check your appearance, etc. If using public transportation, budget even more cushion time. Better to be too early than risk arriving late.

Confirm all logistics in advance - the exact interview time, location, office or floor number, and the full name(s) and title(s) of your interviewer(s). Never assume you know these details.

Once you arrive, be friendly with the security guards, receptionist, and others in the facility. Politely let them know you have arrived for your scheduled interview and identify the person you are there to see.

Use the waiting time before the interview strategically. Review your resume and notes. Mentally rehearse your answers and main talking points. Breathe deeply to stay relaxed. Being a little early removes rush and stress from the process.

For virtual interviews, log on to test your audio/video 2-3 minutes early. Use the remaining moments to center yourself, sit up straight, and glance at your notes.

Arriving early, whether in-person or virtual, makes a responsible and eager impression compared to rushing at the last minute. Show you respect others' time as well as your own. Punctuality signals professionalism.

Andre had a final round interview scheduled for a software engineering role at a prestigious tech company. He knew punctuality would make a strong first impression.

The night before, Andre confirmed the exact office location, floor number, and video conference log-in. Even though he had been in the building before, he didn't assume any details.

On interview day, Andre allotted extra time for traffic delays. He arrived at the building with 10 minutes to spare. In the lobby, Andre reviewed his notes one last time while taking some deep breaths to stay focused. He even did the Suparman Pose in the reflection of the window of his car before walking in.

Andre introduced himself to the receptionist politely and notified her he had arrived for his 1pm interview.

At 1pm sharp, the hiring manager entered the lobby. She smiled warmly at Andre and said, "I appreciate you arriving a few minutes early and being ready to start on time."

During the interview, Andre spoke confidently about his qualifications while maintaining good eye contact. His punctuality had gotten the conversation off on the right foot.

The next day, Andre received a call with an invitation to come in for the final interview with senior management, which ultimately led to an offer. The hiring manager let him know that his professionalism and punctuality throughout the interview process had stood out positively. She looked forward to welcoming him to the team soon.

Here are some activities to help you get started:

- Confirm the exact interview date, time, location, and interviewer names.
- Plan your route and account for extra commute time if needed.
- For virtual interviews, test your computer audio/video ahead of time.
- Pick your interview outfit the night before and have it ready.
- Set multiple alarms in case you oversleep.
- Eat a healthy meal and drink water before the interview.
- Arrive 10-15 minutes early for in-person interviews.
- Notify the receptionist politely when you arrive.
- Use waiting time to review notes and relax.
- For virtual interviews, log on 2-3 minutes early.
- Adjust your camera framing and lighting if needed.
- Sit up straight and breathe deeply before you begin.
- Greet the interviewer with a smile and handshake.

Chapter 7 - Ready, Set, Engage.

Nonverbal communication is just as important as what you say in an interview. Making steady eye contact and smiling helps convey confidence and leaves people with a positive impression.

When first meeting your interviewer, look them in the eyes, smile warmly, and give a firm handshake. This shows you are engaged and happy to be there. Don't have a limp, weak handshake.

Maintain friendly eye contact throughout the interview to show you are actively listening. Avoid looking down or around the room too much. But don't stare intensely either - brief breaks of eye contact are normal.

Smile when appropriate to project a positive, optimistic energy. This will make the conversation feel natural, not overly stiff, or formal. Don't smile constantly or inappropriately. The interviewer will pick up on genuine warmth.

Avoid distracting mannerisms like tapping your foot or clicking a pen. Sit still and focus all your energy into the discussion. Lean slightly forward to display interest.

With the right balance of eye contact, smiling, and engaged body language, you can connect easily with your interviewer and leave a memorable impression.

James had a final round interview for a sales manager position at a large manufacturing company. He knew that confident, engaging body language would make him stand out.

When James met his interviewer, he looked her in the eyes, smiled genuinely, and gave a firm handshake. "It's wonderful to meet you," James said warmly as they sat down.

Throughout the interview, James maintained friendly eye contact to show he was actively listening. He smiled and nodded to put the interviewer at ease.

James sat up straight and leaned in slightly to display interest. He avoided fidgeting or looking around the room.

The interviewer mirrored his behavior and without knowing it, was fully engaged with James. They had a great conversation.

At the end, James thanked the interviewer sincerely while maintaining strong eye contact. His positive body language had reinforced his verbal responses perfectly.

The hiring manager later told the CEO, "James' confident demeanor and captivating communication style really impressed me. He has the presence needed to lead high-stakes sales meetings."

James received the official job offer a week later. His body language had spoken volumes, helping him clinch the role.

<u>Here are some activities to help you get started:</u>

- Practice your handshake to make it confident but not too firm.
- Rehearse smiling naturally and steady eye contact.
- Sit upright and lean in slightly to demonstrate interest.
- Avoid fidgeting - keep hands still and feet on the floor.
- Minimize looking down or around the room too much.
- Nod and make brief comments to confirm your listening.
- Ask a friend to give feedback on your eye contact and demeanor.

Chapter 8 - They're giving it away for free.

Active listening is crucial during a job interview. Give your undivided attention to what the interviewer is saying and asking. If you don't understand a question, politely ask for clarification.

Avoid interrupting or trying to anticipate where the interviewer is going. Let them finish speaking before you respond. Don't just wait for your turn to talk.

Make occasional verbal acknowledgements like "Yes" and "I see" to confirm you are engaged. Nod your head and maintain eye contact as well.

You can take brief notes if that helps you stay focused. Jot down keywords or facts you want to remember to reference later.

If you need a question repeated, politely say something like, "That's interesting, how do you mean?" Don't respond to a question you didn't fully comprehend.

Listening carefully ensures you fully understand the interviewer before crafting your response. You don't want to miss important details or go off tangent. Stay focused and present.

Juan arrived for his interview for a marketing manager role eager to make a strong impression. He knew that active listening would be key.

When the hiring manager asked the first question, Juan maintained steady eye contact and nodded along as she spoke. He avoided interrupting or trying to guess where she was going.

When she finished, Juan briefly summarized her question to confirm his understanding before thoughtfully answering.

Throughout the interview, Juan focused intently on what was being said. He made comments like "I see" and "that's right" to show his attention.

At one point, the interviewer mentioned a complex marketing automation platform. Juan politely asked her to share an example of how they are using it to gather more insight before answering the question.

After the interview, the hiring manager remarked to her colleague "Juan was one of the most engaged listeners I've interviewed. He carefully considered each question before responding thoughtfully. His communication skills will enable him to succeed here."

Juan soon received the job offer. His active listening had shown the sincerity and comprehension needed to ace the interview.

Here are some activities to help you get started:

- Avoid interrupting or jumping ahead - let them fully finish speaking.
- Briefly rephrase or summarize key points to confirm understanding.
- Make brief verbal acknowledgements like "I see" and "That's insightful."
- Take notes if helpful, jotting down key words or themes.
- Politely ask for clarification if you don't fully understand a question.
- Refrain from responding before you are certain you heard the full question.
- Stay focused and present - don't let your mind wander.
- Ask a friend to practice interviewing you and provide feedback.

Chapter 9 - Leave it all on the table.

Your verbal delivery is key to answering interview questions confidently. Speak slowly, clearly, and deliberately. Avoid rushing through your responses.

Phrase statements directly rather than raising questions. For example, "I successfully led that project by doing X, Y and Z" rather than, "I think I successfully led that project?"

Provide specific examples and data to back up claims when possible. Facts and figures strengthen your responses. It is essential to quantify your achievements.

It's completely fine to pause and collect your thoughts before responding. Silence for a few seconds is better than rambling.

Avoid filler words like "um" and "like." Speak professionally, not casually. But don't become too stiff or use words that aren't natural for you either.

Keep your volume at an appropriate level - not too loud or too quiet. Enunciate properly and avoid mumbling.

With preparation and practice, you can enter the interview with the confidence to articulate your experience and qualifications persuasively.

Mark had a final interview for a sales director role at a premiere sporting goods company. He knew his verbal delivery would impact how his qualifications were perceived.

When asked about his leadership experience, Mark spoke slowly and clearly. He provided a specific example, stating "I successfully exceeded our sales goals by implementing a new CRM system for our team."

Mark spoke with conviction, making direct statements about his achievements. He avoided sounding unsure or peppering his responses with unnecessary filler words.

When asked a challenging question, Mark paused for a few seconds to thoughtfully consider his response. He maintained good eye contact all the while.

The interviewer later commented to her boss, "Mark's confident communication style and thoughtful responses really impressed me. He speaks like a leader who can steer key client conversations effectively."

In the follow-up call with the job offer, the hiring manager mentioned how Mark's polished, yet natural verbal delivery solidified him as the top candidate. Focusing on his communication skills had clearly paid off.

<u>Here are some activities to help you get started:</u>

- Speak slowly and clearly - avoid rushing through responses.
- Make direct statements about your background and qualifications.
- Provide specific examples and data when possible, to strengthen responses.
- Pause briefly before responding if needed to collect your thoughts.
- Avoid filler words like "um", "uh", and "like".
- Practice answering questions out loud to polish delivery.
- Strike a balance between professional but natural language.
- Keep the volume at an appropriate level - don't mumble.
- Make eye contact and nod to engage the interviewer while speaking.

Chapter 10 – You Know what you Know.

Honesty and integrity are always key in interviews. If you don't know the answer to a question, don't try to fake it. It's better to be upfront.

For example, if asked about an unfamiliar software program or task, respond politely with, "I don't have direct experience with that, but I'd be very interested to learn more." If you have experience with a similar system, you can mention that too help bridge the gap.

Then, follow up by emphasizing your willingness to ask questions and ability to quickly pick up new skills. Demonstrating interest and a passion for learning can be just as valuable as already knowing the answer. Admitting what you don't know also builds trust.

While you want to focus on your strengths in an interview, don't exaggerate abilities or make false claims. Use good judgment and be as truthful as possible. Your character matters.

Arun had an interview for a data analyst position at a financial firm. One area he had limited experience in was with Power BI, a specific data visualization software mentioned in the job description.

When asked about his experience with Power BI, Arun politely responded "I don't have direct experience with that program, but I pick up new data tools very quickly. My background is in Salesforce and Tableau, which are similar tools. I'd be excited to learn Power BI if needed for this role."

The interviewer nodded and said "I appreciate your honesty. We can train the right candidate in Power BI if needed. Eagerness to learn new skills is valuable here."

Later, the hiring manager told the team "I was impressed by Arun's transparency when asked about Power BI. He could have tried to exaggerate his abilities, but his honesty and enthusiasm to learn stood out."

Arun soon received the job offer. While he was still building expertise in certain areas, his integrity gave the company confidence he was the right person to take a chance on.

Here are some activities to help you get started:

- If asked about something unfamiliar, politely acknowledge you don't have direct experience.
- Emphasize eagerness to learn new skills and ability to pick things up quickly.
- Offer examples of other similar skills that will help you get up to speed.
- Mention your willingness to research and get back with more details.
- Focus on highlighting your strengths, but don't exaggerate abilities.
- Admit openly if you are still building capabilities in certain areas.
- Maintain a sincere tone - don't appear evasive or defensive.

Chapter 11 - The Moment of Truth

Make sure to prepare several thoughtful questions to ask the interviewer, as an interview is a two-way conversation.

It's important to start the interview by asking the specific question, "What was it about my resume that you liked?" End the question on the word "liked" - do not rephrase it. This gets the interviewer talking about your strengths right away and reveals what they prioritize.

Listen closely to their response for insights you can incorporate into your answers later. Ask appropriate follow-up questions to show your engagement.

In addition, prepare other smart questions that demonstrate your curiosity and interest in learning more about the role and company.

For example, you could ask:

- What are the day-to-day responsibilities of this role?
- How would you describe the work culture here?
- What do you enjoy most about working for this company?

Even if the interviewer already covered the topics you planned to ask about, express appreciation for their thoroughness. End by reinforcing your enthusiasm.

Well-chosen questions make the interview a thoughtful, two-way conversation and leave a positive impression. Starting with "What was it about my resume that you liked?" gets it off on the right foot.

When Eric arrived for his project manager interview, he was prepared with thoughtful questions, starting with a specific opener.

After some introductory discussion, Eric politely asked "What was it about my resume that you liked?" focusing on the word "liked" just as he had practiced.

The interviewer smiled and said "Great question! I was really impressed by your wide range of technical experience and the data analytics project you led. That combined with your career growth and leadership responsibilities makes your resume stand out. Those skills will serve you well here."

Eric asked smart follow-up questions tailored to those areas, demonstrating his engagement. The interviewer was nodding along pleased with the meaningful dialogue.

At the end, Eric expressed his appreciation for the interviewer's time and insights. As he was leaving, the interviewer remarked "Eric clearly did his research on effective interview techniques. His strategic questions yielded a productive discussion."

In the follow-up call with the job offer, the hiring manager referenced their meaningful dialogue and Eric's well-prepared questions focused on his strengths. His thorough preparation had shown impressive strategic insight.

<u>Here are some activities to help you get started:</u>

- Start with a specific opener like "What was it about my resume that you liked?"
- Listen actively for insights you can incorporate into your responses.
- Ask smart follow-up questions to get more detail.
- Make sure questions demonstrate knowledge and interest.
- Adjust questions based on what has already been covered.

Chapter 12 - Gratitude

Always thank the interviewer for their time at the end of the interview. Shake hands, make eye contact, and reaffirm your enthusiasm for the role.

For example, "Thank you for taking the time to meet today. It was wonderful learning more about the role and company. I'm very excited about the opportunity."

Follow up within 24 hours by emailing each interviewer, referring to something specific you discussed. Briefly reiterate your interest and qualifications for the job.

Thanking the interviewer properly leaves your interaction on a positive note and gets you remembered. With some genuine appreciation, you can continue nurturing the relationship even after the interview is over.

Towards the end of Sarah's marketing manager interview, the hiring manager asked, "Do you have any final questions for me?"

Sarah smiled and said "No, you've been very thorough in explaining the role, which I appreciate. Based on our conversation, I'm even more excited about the position and confident I would be a great fit."

The interviewer nodded, "Excellent, I'm glad you're interested."

Sarah concluded, "Thank you again for taking so much time to meet with me today. It was a pleasure learning more about this opportunity."

They stood up and Sarah gave a firm handshake, maintaining eye contact.

The next day, Sarah sent a thank you email referencing a past successful marketing campaign they had discussed, reiterating her enthusiasm.

A week later, the hiring manager called Sarah with the job offer, mentioning how much she appreciated Sarah's thoughtful closing questions and prompt follow-up.

Sarah's genuine appreciation and consistency in nurturing the relationship had made her memorable after the interview ended, helping seal the deal.

Here are some activities to help you get started:

- Express sincere thanks for the interviewer's time and insights.
- Shake hands firmly while maintaining eye contact when leaving.
- Reaffirm your interest and confidence in being a great fit.
- Follow up within 24 hours by email to thank them again.
- Reference something specific discussed that resonated with you.
- Briefly reiterate your top qualifications and enthusiasm.
- Customize thank you notes if you interviewed with multiple people.
- Send handwritten notes if appropriate and feasible.

CONCLUSION

Landing your dream job starts with a stellar interview. While interviews can seem daunting, preparation is the key to unlocking success. Arm yourself with research to tailor compelling responses. Practice until you can smoothly articulate your qualifications and enthusiasm. Dress sharply to convey professionalism and make a great first impression with polite confidence.

This guide has equipped you with strategies to help control interview nerves and shine under pressure. From thoughtful questions to memorable closing remarks, you now have proven tips to ace every stage of the interview process.

Remember, interviews are a two-way street. While making a strong case for yourself, also determine if the role is an ideal fit. Listen closely for signs of the company culture and work align with your values and goals.

With dedication to continuous learning and growth, any position can become your dream job. So, walk into interviews with optimism and wisdom. Believe in your worth and abilities. With the preparation and passion this guide has stoked, you are ready to impress hiring managers and get hired. Go make your next interview your best one yet!

ABOUT THE AUTHOR

Ben Passman brings a unique blend of broadcasting, military service, business ownership, and recruiting experience to his readers. Ben served in the U.S. Navy prior to entering college, where he won several awards for broadcasting excellence while earning his Communication and Journalism degree from the University of New Mexico.

In 2008, Ben leveraged his skills to transition into talent acquisition, recruiting for various high-growth companies. During the COVID-19 pandemic, Ben expanded his passion for guiding professionals by hosting the podcast "A Peek Behind the Curtain" where he provided weekly job search tips and career insights.

Now Ben helps job seekers transform their trajectories through his revamped podcast "Dream Job Equation" and customized career acceleration programs. Drawing from over a decade of recruiting and HR experience, Ben empowers clients to showcase their value, align with purpose, and secure fulfilling roles.

When he isn't coaching individuals or speaking at industry events, Ben shares his insider perspective on the modern job search through his blog, and social media.